SOUTH KOREA 101

The Culture, Etiquette, Rules and Customs

MANCHO SOTO

About The Author:

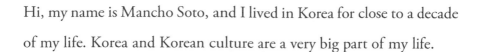

Hi, my name is Mancho Soto, and I lived in Korea for close to a decade of my life. Korea and Korean culture are a very big part of my life.

I usually joke that I'm half-Korean. I spent most of my 20's in South Korea. Now, I live in Fort Lee, NJ, which is a town in New Jersey that has a very high Korean population. Last, my wife is a native of Daegu, Korea.

Why should I even bring it up? The reason I bring this up is because I want to express that the information contained in this book is all from first-hand experience. The reason I wrote it is because I wanted to share something that I believe in and something that I feel will help people interested in Korea and in Korean culture improve their knowledge and their lives. Having knowledge of the Korean culture can be beneficial to those looking to live in Korea, work with Koreans, or in general, to have Korean friends. It will also be helpful for those who want to understand the Korean mind better. I think Korea is a fantastic country that has a lot to offer. My main goal here is to share information on South Korea to bring more exposure to this fantastic country.

I think that having lived in Korea has greatly enhanced my life. I think you may experience a similar result!

South Korea 101: The Culture, Etiquette, Rules and Customs

1) In Korea, the Chinese characters are very important. While learning Korean, you should learn the meaning of some of the individual Chinese characters. For example, the word *mi-gook*, which means America, is a combination of *mi* (beautiful) *gook* (country.) This lesson I learned through my Korean friend Jane, who once said to me, "My dad always told me that, when I look up a new word in the dictionary, I should also learn the Chinese character associated with it."

2) Most Korean names have meanings. If you ask someone, "What does your name mean?", they will give you an answer such as "Beauty and Wise". When you begin to learn people's names and when you can remember their significance, they will be very happy. If when meeting someone, you can guess their name's meaning, they will be very excited and impressed that you know some Chinese characters.

3) In Korea, special emphasis is placed on people's skin. There is a reason women regularly wear facial masks before going to bed. Many men, although fewer than women, will wear facial masks as well. When in Korea, I used to get a facial every other

week. People are very complimentary. When you have bad skin, people are really blunt and can be hurtful.

4) I was born in 1981. According to the Chinese Zodiac, that is the year of the Rooster. Since the Chinese Zodiac has 12 different animal signs, you can tell someone's age by their animal sign. If someone is also a rooster, but younger than me, I know they were born in 1993, 2005 or 2017. If they are older than me, perhaps they were born in 1969 or 1957. You can ask someone their age by asking their Chinese Zodiac. This is super-Korean.

How to use: Let's say you were born in 1999. You look up your Chinese Zodiac, and you will see that you are a Rabbit. In a conversation, you can say, "What Animal Sign are you? I am a Rabbit. I was born in 1999." Then your conversation partner will tell you their Sign. Keep in mind that, in most cases, Koreans will want to know your age.

5) One characteristic of the Korean language is that there is formal and informal language. You will usually use formal language. As a general rule, people use formal language with one another when they are not close. As they get to know one another, the older person will speak informally to the younger person, but the younger person will speak formally to the older person. This indicates a sign of respect to one's elders.

This is very important: Koreans don't know how to speak to one another unless they know one another's age. Therefore, very early in the relationship, they will ask "How old are you?" Until this matter is settled, they don't really know how to talk to one another. Don't be surprised if people ask you your age *immediately after* finding out your name.

6) Sejong the Great King is a big hero. When I moved to Korea in 2005, there was still a holiday that celebrated the founding of *Hangeul,* the Korean alphabet or characters. *Hangeul* was so well made that a foreigner, such as myself, could learn to read out the sounds (not understanding words) within a couple of hours of study. You could also do the same if you ask someone to teach you. This is largely thanks to Sejong the Great King, who had scholars create this great writing system for their language. Prior to having a written language of their own, Koreans relied on Chinese characters to express their thoughts. It worked quite well, but there is nothing like having your own language represented by your own script or writing.

In essence, Sejong the Great King allowed Koreans to express themselves more naturally. Also, the Korean alphabet is much easier to learn than Chinese characters. Many more Koreans were able to read and write after the creation of the Korean alphabet.

Cool fact: Sejong the Great King appears in the 10,000 won bill, which was the highest denomination bill for many years. His significance is shown by having his image on the Korean won, and there are numerous roads and statues named after him.

7) One phrase you will hear often in Korea is "Pali Pali". This translates to "Fast, Fast". Mothers use it to tell their kids to come quickly. Other people use it to urge someone on, basically to put the *pedal to the metal*. I think it's important to know this because I call Korea a "Pali Pali" culture. Everyone has expectations for others to get things done quickly.

The impressive thing is that delivery of food or online products is usually very fast. Whenever you need something fixed, a repair person can be there the same day. This is the good of the "Pali Pali" mindset.

If you want to install cable or internet in your house, they will come to your house the same day.

This mindset has made Korean people a bit impatient. That's why everyone crowds around the bus's doors, vying to go in first, instead of forming a line. Furthermore, sometimes on the street, hurried people will bump into you *without apology* and hurry away. They are just thinking about getting to their destination quickly. This is the bad of the "Pali Pali" mindset.

Overall, the good far outweighs the bad when it comes to the "Pali Pali" culture.

How to use: When your friend is taking a little longer than expected, you can urge them on jokingly and say, "Pali Pali".

Most likely, they will laugh and think you have learned the culture well.

8) Koreans are good at drawing from all the doodling they do in their after-school academies.

What would you like to do after school? If you're like me, the answer given is, "Not more school."

Most Korean teens have to spend their after-school time at more schooling via private academies or home tutoring. This over-saturation of lessons can lead to their focus being diminished. In order to deal with this information overload, Korean students allow their minds to drift. Sometimes, they will doodle. Through the years of mentally drifting and doodling, Koreans actually build their artistic skills.

This by no means applies to everyone, and this does not mean the average Korean is an art prodigy. But *I do believe* the average Korean may be better at drawing from all the time spent doodling in the academies.

9) In Korea, *public transportation is amazing.* There are many taxis that you can take, and they are relatively cheap. Also, the subway system is clean, efficient, and easy to use. If you want to travel between cities, I would recommend travel via the KTX or Korean high-speed bullet train. The KTX traverses most of the major locations throughout the country. Most citizens' transportation needs can be met via public transportation.

Throughout my 9 years in Korea, I never owned a car, and I never felt a need to own one.

10) South Korea is not a major bicycle-riding country. When I visited the city of Fukuoka in Japan, which is very close to Busan, I noticed that many more people ride bicycles there. In fact, walking out of my hotel, I almost got run over by a bicycle. I have also read that, in Beijing, China, many people use bikes as a major source of transportation. In Korea, very few people ride bicycles. I think what's more common are the little purple scooters that a delivery person will ride.

11) South Korea is a bowing country-meaning that bows are often used for different reasons. People bow all the time to say

"Hello". Usually, people will bow and say "Annyung-Haseyo". This is the most common greeting.

You also bow when you are sorry. You bow and say "I'm sorry". You also bow when you say "Goodbye". When you are the person leaving a location, you say "Stay in Peace". When someone is leaving your place, then you say, "Go in peace".

Regardless, there will be a lot of bowing. If you stay in Korea a long time, you will likely bow your head on a regular basis with no conscious effort.

12) Here's a practical tip: Say someone's last name first and first name last.

For example: My name is Mancho Soto, but in Korea, I am Soto, Mancho.

So, when I go to a doctor's office, they will call me Soto, Mancho when calling for me.

When you call for someone on the street, call them like this: Kim, Minji.

This way is super-Korean, and Koreans will know you are a pro with their culture.

13) You should NOT write a person's name in red ink. This is a common superstition. Koreans will think you want them to die. It's believed that, if your name is written in red ink, then you will soon die. I think the redness brings about an association with blood. You will notice quickly if you try to write someone's name in red ink, one of your Korean friends will recommend that you use blue or black ink instead so as not to offend or scare the person whose name you are writing.

14) Alcohol etiquette:

As the receiver: When you have a glass and someone is pouring you some alcohol, you should hold your glass or cup with 2 hands. This is proper etiquette in Korea.

As the pourer: When pouring or offering someone a glass of alcohol, you pour with your dominant hand. Your weak hand should be placed on the dominant arm's elbow. This is proper alcohol etiquette. You should not pour without regard. This is considered rude. For some reason, alcohol etiquette is a big part of the Korean culture.

15) You must take off your shoes when entering a home in Korea. To avoid embarrassment, make sure your *socks are in decent shape,* meaning there are no holes in them, and preferably, they would be a matching pair. Koreans believe that shoes are dirty. I would have to agree with them. Although I now live in the

US, I still keep the practice of taking off my shoes at the door immediately after entering my house.

Also, you will normally find indoor slippers for you to use at the front door. There will also be a separate pair of bathroom slippers outside the bathroom. These are made of material that can get wet. Whereas the regular indoor slippers should not get wet because then you're just going to be left with wet feet. If you want to follow the Korean household's way, you should keep both types of slippers for yourself and for your guests.

16) There is proper etiquette for giving and getting money. When you are handing someone money, such as the monthly tuition for a private tutor, you should *give the money* <u>inside an enclosed envelope.</u>

If you receive an envelope of money, you should receive it *with both hands*.

More on money: If you are paying cash at a shop or supermarket, you don't put it in an envelope, but you do put one hand on your elbow while extending the other hand holding the cash.

Whenever you receive cash, it should be with two hands. You will be considered rude if you just do a one-handed grab.

17) I recommend learning the Korean language. It is a commitment, but if you're going to spend more than 6 months in the country, then I would recommend learning the language. There are many benefits. The best way is to ask a Korean friend to teach you how to read Korean.

If you learn how to read, then you can learn every day from the street signs or while ordering food or drinks at restaurants. You will become a learning machine and you will have a much richer experience.

However, if you're not that interested in learning the language, then you will be able to learn the culture and history through English. There are many English-speaking Koreans, who would love to share their culture with you.

Bonus tip: If you decide to take on the task of learning the Korean language, I would strongly recommend that, each time you look up a new Korean word, you should play the audio of it in order to remember it better and to capture the correct pronunciation.

18) You should get used to eating spicy food gradually. I love Korean food, but when I first arrived in Korea, about 80% of the food I found to be too spicy for me. Even my first breakfast with my home stay family included *spicy food*-**FOR BREAKFAST!**

I was shocked. I could not even fathom why someone would serve spicy food for breakfast. Over time, I developed the capability to handle eating spicy food. Now I enjoy having some spice in my food.

This is something that should be developed over time. If you want to enjoy your time eating in Korea, it would be helpful to build a tolerance for spiciness.

Tips on how to lower hotness: One way to get better at eating spiciness is to mix the spicy food with the rice. *You WILL have rice.* There is no shortage of rice in Korea. You put the spicy food with the rice, and that blend should diminish the overall amount of spice that hits you.

19) If you are in Korea, I would also check out traveling within Korea. Obviously, Seoul has a lot to offer. I would encourage you to visit other cities as well and even go to some small towns. The small towns may be boring, but sometimes they can offer you a breather or a refresher. I liked to explore different museums, temples, and landmarks, as well as local markets, and I enjoyed having conversations with local people.

20) Try the Korean *street cart food*. Some of it is tasty, and most of it is relatively inexpensive. You will get to know the local people in your neighborhood if you visit at the same time regularly.

The more people you know, the easier it is to make friends and build relationships.

I became friends with a local vendor of custard-filled snacks. She and her boyfriend were always so kind to me. Since her food cart was at a busy neighborhood corner, I would greet them regularly. Just saying "Hello" sometimes adds to your day. It makes you feel like part of the neighborhood.

Recommendations: I like sweet snacks, so I would enjoy having some *Hotteok*. Many Koreans love *Tteokbokki*, so they will recommend it perhaps, but I wouldn't order it yet. I would try one of my Korean friend's snacks when they order. It is spicy, so it's better to try carefully, especially if you can't handle spicy foods well.

21) Learn about K-pop, Korean TV shows and movies. This is one of the best ways to learn the language and culture all wrapped in one. Also, this puts you in-the-know, and it helps you build relationships with people. Knowing what's going on with pop-culture will make you more relatable. This will be helpful in building relations and shows an appreciation for the creativity of the culture. Liking the Korean culture will also help Koreans like you more.

22) Learn ways that Koreans are funny. Listen to what makes Koreans laugh. You can replicate this and be funny. Just follow the laughs.

23) If you take on the task of learning Korean, make sure you make it a daily practice. You don't have to be as hardcore as I was, but consistency and practice are key. My first 6 months in Korea, I made it a habit of studying around 4 hours a day. I never had any formal training. My Korean friend Jane taught me the alphabet, and I just ran with it. I always found language learning fun, so it was not tedious to me. Your natural inclination for language-learning and your will to learn the language will determine how much time you want to put towards learning the language. I came to Korea with the intention of doing business or living long-term, so I knew that learning the language was the first step to living a great life in a foreign country.

Personal Note: My parents immigrated to the US from Colombia in 1981 with me. That is the year I was born. My parents raised me as a typical Colombian boy in a town called Middletown, NY.

Nobody spoke English in my family. I was raised in a Spanish-speaking household and didn't speak a word of English when I entered Pre-

Kindergarten. In a span of two to three years, I finally found myself being able to communicate with classmates in English.

My parents worked mostly manual labor job, such as working in factories. They worked in jobs as laborers, and I don't think there was much opportunity to learn English, let alone a high level of English at those jobs. My dad continued down this path until retirement. Even until his last days, he didn't feel that comfortable speaking in English.

However, on the other hand, my mom attended Boces, which offered a program on English as a 2nd Language. This was ten years after already having lived in the US only knowing Spanish.

I must have been in about 5th grade in elementary school. I remember that, at that time, she would stay up at night studying English. After one year of studying, she was able to enter Orange County Community College in Middletown, NY. She was thrilled. Through much effort, she graduated with an Associate's Degree. Through this herculean effort, she managed to land a low-paying office job where she worked as a bookkeeper. She radiated with pride working in an office where most labor was mental and not physical. I saw her confidence grow through her ability to learn English. I could see her head was lifted higher thereafter.

This must have stuck with me because, from Day 1, I was determined to learn Korean. I knew that, if I wanted to do anything major in the country, I would need the language.

Incidentally, growing up bilingual with Spanish and English, I was exposed to different sounds, structures, and sentence patterns. The vowel sounds found in Spanish aided me tremendously with the vowel sounds made in Korean. Language, which was once my weakness, suddenly became one of my main strengths. Also, from this personal experience, I learned that *knowledge of a language is potential power.*

24) After I studied for six or seven months straight, I found a way to super-boost my Korean language learning. I had a few go-to coffee shops where I would go to study on the weekends. I went to one of the coffee shops maybe 3 or 4 consecutive weekends. Since it was a small coffee shop, the owner worked there, and she had a few part-time employees helping her. She was always there. One weekend, however, she wasn't there. I asked the part-time worker where the boss was. She asked me, "Do you want to see the boss?" with kind of a mischievous giggle. I thought, and I was about to lie and say "No." But I said, "What the hell? Yes, I do want to see the boss." She giggled.

Looking back, I think this conversation must have been relayed to the boss.

The following week, I was studying in that same coffee shop when the boss came and served me a cheesecake "on the house." I thanked her and continued studying. After studying there two or three hours, she came back to me and asked, "Do you want to go for a drive?" She pointed at her convertible Audi. Again, I thought about it for a split-second, and I said "What the hell? Let's go."

After that time and a few dates later, we began dating.

She owned the coffee shop, and she was an older Korean woman. She happened to not speak any English. Had I not put in the early work learning Korean all those months by myself, there would have been no relationship. We communicated, traveled, and explored the country all in Korean.

We dated for about a year, and my Korean Language ability sky-rocketed during that time.

Dating in Korea will boost your knowledge of the culture, language, and etiquette!

25) In Korea, if you are an English-speaker, people who are interested in outside cultures and who are interested in you will come to you. You will attract those who are interested in you and repel those uninterested in you. There is less diversity in Korea, so most likely, if you are an English-speaker, your

presence will attract attention. *People will seek you.* The challenge is not looking for people to talk with you, in most cases. The challenge will be finding who you want to talk to out of those people that seek you.

For example, one common practice that I often used is, I would study in a public place mainly to get out of the house, develop myself, and be in front of people. I would usually go to a book store *with a café or just a stand-alone cafe.* This was, in my opinion, the best way to meet people. I was studying, which I loved to do, and I would do it in public, which surrounded me with like-minded people.

First, I would not sit in a central location because it decreases the chance of conversation in my opinion. I think that people are less likely to start a conversation. Usually, I would sit in the back where there was more privacy. I figured that it would be easier to have a conversation and possibly make a new friend. If not, then at least it would be quiet, and I would be able to further my studies or reading.

Second, I would carry a Korean language learning book and a book in English just so I could alternate back and forth and keep my interest and focus level high. I would study a good hour straight. This is all it takes to meet people in Korea.

In the meantime, another café customer would sit beside me. Usually, the person or people sitting next to me would be studying as well.

My theory is that people that sit next to you in that situation will have a higher likelihood of being interested in foreign cultures or languages. You are already there, and they are the ones who decide to sit next to you. After studying for a while, I would go on a bathroom break. I would leave my books there on the table. (In Korea, this is very common because it's a really safe country, and we're talking about leaving books on the table, not Gold!)

Upon returning from the bathroom, I would often arrive back at the table where I was seated, and after making eye contact, I would greet the person, "Hello." They would say something along the lines, "I see that you study Korean. Do you like Korea?" This was always a great way to start a conversation with little to no effort all while learning what I wanted to learn. I highly recommend using this strategy with sincerity and with a mindset of wanting to learn and wanting to meet people.

Personal Note:

———◇◦◇———

I started the practice of studying in public in Korea after recalling a practice used by Benjamin Franklin. In his autobiography, he wrote that, early in his business career, he would make sure that he was seen in public late in the evening still working so that he would gain a reputation for being industrious. He thought this helped him gain in reputation and later in actual business.

I think that I also wanted to gain a reputation for being hard-working in Korea. In this study-culture, one major way to be respected is to be seen as a serious scholar. Therefore, I would often go to a local Starbucks or Korean coffee shop, and I would study. Oftentimes, I became known there, and people would want to speak with me. This would also help with teaching as I gained many private lesson students this way. After parents recognized how serious I was about studying and learning, they often made the conclusion that I would make a great teacher for themselves or for their children. I did absolutely *No marketing in Korea*. All the private study students that I gained were obtained in this manner *or through referrals*. I did not know anything about sales or how to market while living in Korea. I never asked anyone if they needed a teacher. All the students that I gained just came to me. I rarely spent any time at home. I was in a public space as often as possible, and I simply studied and talked with people that were interested in talking with me.

This is not just about teaching and gaining students. This is more about presenting yourself in a favorable manner to a given culture or group of people. I'm not sure if it can work for you, but it definitely worked for me in Korea.

26) Most Non-Koreans spend most of their time in South Korea with other Non-Koreans. Now, I live in New Jersey. Most Korean immigrants also spend most of their time with other Koreans. When I lived in Middletown, New York, my parents who were from Colombia mostly or wholly spent their time with other Colombians. This is very common. *If you want to learn about Korea and Korean culture, you have to spend lots of time with Koreans.* This is something that almost everyone knows, but very few people practice. In order to learn the culture, you have to stop surrounding yourself exclusively with people from your own culture.

Now, I'm going to encourage you to do both. You should meet people from within your culture because it's great to joke around and have conversations with others who can really understand each and every word you speak. I like that, too.

At the same time, the goal here is also to understand the Korean culture. In order for you to do that, you must meet Korean people, plain and simple.

27) If you want to fit into the culture, I would use Samsung and LG products. Koreans are very proud of their country, and there is a sort of patriotism when it comes to electronic goods and phones.

There was a time when Korean products were very behind Japanese products. Those days, Koreans who wanted top quality electronics were forced to purchase Japanese goods. Those days are long gone. Now, many Korean goods are of equal or greater quality than their Japanese counterparts. To this day, many Koreans choose to buy domestic products to support the domestic companies, which in turn, helps their own economy.

Considering that many Koreans have this mindset, when you own Samsung or LG, you are thinking like them. I was asked on numerous occasions, "Do you have an iPhone or a Samsung phone?" When I replied, "I like to support the country where I'm living, so I have a Samsung phone," my Korean friends became very happy. They usually thought and said that I was very much like a Korean. I took this as a compliment.

28) In Korea, one of the favorite pastimes is singing Karaoke with friends. In America, we hardly ever sing. I remember I took chorus in middle school just because a few cute girls were taking it. I had *NO interest* in singing. That's a shame because I could surely have used it in Korea. There were *MANY* gatherings where singing could have helped me. Singing to Koreans is like Salsa dancing to Colombians. It is not a necessity in the culture, but it helps especially in social events. When you are in Latin America, learning dance is a practical skill.

In Korea, *singing is that practical social skill.*

In Korea, people of all ages- teenagers, college students, and adults, _all enjoy singing_. If you are in Korea a few months, you will be asked to go to a **Norae Bang**, which literally means "Song Room". This Karaoke or "Norae Bang" offers an opportunity for you to let loose and show that you are not only good at studying or at work. You can really have fun and make friends with greater ease if you have fun the way it's done in the culture.

For the first several years, I was reluctant to go because I was too shy about singing. You don't have to even sing. You can rap, sing, or dance. The main point is to show that you have fun within the Korean culture. Don't get me wrong. The more you practice, the better your singing will be.

This is why the average Korean is a much better singer than the average American, in my opinion. Ask the average Korean to sing a song, and I'm pretty sure they have a few songs they will gladly sing. Ask the same question to an American friend, and they will not know which song to sing.

It's a matter of practice. Don't wait years before enjoying the "Norae Bang" like I did. In order to enjoy your time in Korea, I would encourage you to challenge yourself and accept the invitation from a Korean friend. Go to the "Norae Bang" and sing a song. At least you are amongst friends or soon to be friends. Sing your heart out!

This is a great way to make friends in Korea and in any other country for that matter.

29) In Korea, you *will sit on the floor* cross-legged very often. If you ever visit friends or if you ever go to a Korean restaurant, you may find yourself asked to sit down on the floor. This is the traditional way to sit in Korea. Koreans are used to sitting on the floor. If you find this difficult, you may want to eat at restaurants that offer western-style tables and seating. Some restaurants offer both, and you can elect to sit in seating with high tables and chairs.

Another option is that you can stretch before and during your sitting cross-legged session. After some time, it will undoubtedly become easier.

Also, consider this: When you *imagine someone practicing yoga*, how do you envision them?

They may be in a similar pose or position. One option is to take up yoga while in Korea. This can help you *in and out* of the restaurants. It may be a way to "Kill two birds with one stone."

30) In the summertime, you may be awoken by a loud noise that sounds like the musical instrument the *maraca*. There is a distinct rattling sound in the early mornings of hot Korean summer days. You will hear it as you walk outside past the trees. This sound comes from cicadas, an insect that was unbeknownst to me until I first visited Korea. They are locally called "**memi**". These "*memi*" or cicadas are known to grow and nourish underground for years and years. Then, they are aboveground and able to move about, sing and scream for only a few days or weeks before dying. During this short life, they try to make as much noise as possible to find a mate before they die. These are desperate insects. They are probably not too

concerned about you waking up. They are just happy to be alive.

31) Classifications of people in Korea and their meaning from a Korean's point of view:

Foreigner- When Koreans say the word foreigner, they usually imagine a white, blue-eyed person from an English-speaking North American country not named Mexico-mainly American or Canadian. I fell in this category, even though my family is from Colombia. Appearance overrides everything in Korea.

Black- Usually, Koreans will refer to a person who is black as black regardless of whether they are Brazilian, Jamaican, American or from Ghana or the Ivory Coast. It does not matter.

Korean-If you are Asian and your parents, grandparents or great-grand parents and so on were of Korean descent, then you are Korean regardless of whether you grew up in Korea, Argentina, Australia, or Germany. Even if you know no Korean but you "look Korean", you will be considered Korean. Obviously, you are also Korean if your parents are Korean and you are born and raised in Korea.

Other foreigners- You will probably be classified as a foreigner with an emphasis that you are from Russia, France, Spain or another country.

South-East Asian-If you are from Vietnam, Laos, Thailand, Philippines, Indonesia, or other Asian countries, you will be referred to as a South-East Asian in Korea. I think that people from India, Pakistan, and Bangladesh would also fall in this category.

Japanese- You will be referred to as Japanese if you are from Japan.

Chinese- You will be referred to as Chinese if you are from China.

Please note the last two on that list. Japanese people are called Japanese, and Chinese people are called Chinese. The reason they have their own names is because Korea has had a long history with each of these countries. They named them from their dealings with them. They were very familiar with one another; therefore, they were given distinct names. Korea did not have an established trading history with other individual nations; therefore, they were classified vaguely and without accuracy.

This classification system is just my thoughts on how Koreans view different races or nations of people. The general rule is that it's largely based on your skin color. This is how I interpret the way Koreans view other people. Obviously, I may be wrong, but this is my interpretation that I've formed over time mainly living almost 10 years in Korea. I do hope that the classifications become less general and more accurate. Then again, it's just better to go out and meet all types of people and get to know them and see if you want to be friends. Then you can really classify them as someone you want to be friends with or not, regardless of their outer appearance.

I didn't like my classification because there was no acknowledgement of my Colombian background. However, more and more Koreans have been traveling and are becoming more knowledgeable with regard to other countries. A lot of the classifications are more of a generalization. Similarly, my Colombian family had no idea about different countries within Asia. They ignorantly thought that all Asians were *Chinos*, which is how you say *Chinese people* in Spanish. I was also ignorant of other cultures. Luckily, I'm a curious individual, and I studied, asked questions, and met people from diverse backgrounds.

Also, times are changing, and I feel as more international couples are formed, there will be greater acknowledgement of other cultures and people.

> 32) It may be a good idea to make a business card while you are in Korea. It is very common for people to ask you upon meeting, "Do you have a business card or name card?"

You can also do the same and ask someone that question after you first meet them.

Helpful Tip: In Korea, it is a good practice to receive a business card with both hands. Also, you should study the card carefully and put it somewhere with care. This is especially true if you want to leave a good impression. You can show that you understand the culture.

33) Don't give any tips. Don't lay out the cash after getting a haircut. Don't give any extra cash to the taxi driver. Don't leave money on the table for the waitress. Don't give the delivery people (tip) money when they drop off your furniture. Don't give tips. It is weird in Korea.

Helpful Tip: If you do move houses in Korea and use a moving company, which you should if you have lots of furniture, you should buy them lunch. This is common practice. Usually noodles or something they can eat easily is a good choice.

34) I recommend always carrying a book in Korea. You may get stuck somewhere, and it's always good to be learning. If we can participate in something hands-on or if we can join a group, then great. However, if you are in someplace waiting and feel bored, then you can take out your book and join a different world. Keep in mind also that Koreans really respect scholars.

35) If you do learn the Korean language and you want to impress someone, use your knowledge of Chinese characters. However,

if you want to be even more impressive, then use Chinese 4-Character idioms. These idioms all consist of 4 characters.

Let's go over a couple of Chinese 4-character idioms.

These idioms both contain *birds* in them.

A) Birds of a feather flock together: Yu-Yu-Sang-Jong (like and like get together)

B) Kill two birds with one stone: il-Seok-i-Jo (one stone two birds)

Most Koreans know just a few since the origin often comes from the Chinese language. However, most adults in Korea know these *4-character idioms* can be very powerful.

Practical Tip: You don't have to know all of them. Even just learning, memorizing, and using the ones that I mentioned above will get you a lot of respect and credibility in Korea.

This may actually be more advanced. It may be better to focus on learning basics in Korean. I just want you to be informed of the relationship between Korean Language and the Chinese Language.

36) Learn to eat the Korean staples: Bean-paste stew and Kimchi stew. They are often served in a shared bowl. You should get

used to sharing food and eating from the same stew, with each person using their spoons and re-dipping into the same bowl.

If you get used to this, you will have a much easier time fitting in in Korea. Those two foods, bean-paste stew (***DangJang Jigae***) and kimchi stew (***Kimchi Jigae***), are amongst the most classic Korean dishes. If you learn to eat and appreciate these dishes, you will be welcomed in most Korean kitchens, since these are classics of the Korean cuisine.

37) The highest denomination of Korean money is a 50,000 won bill. The chosen person is Shin Saimdang. She was famous for her work in art, literature, and calligraphy. However, she is also known as "the wise mother" because she raised children that were renowned for their learning and contributions to philosophy and art. I think this is really important because many Koreans believe their success is due largely in part to *the focus on education.*

Since there are relatively few natural resources in Korea, Koreans believe *they are the natural resource.* They have to sell the knowledge, skills, and products they create. There is no oil, nor are there any diamond or gold mines in Korea. Most of their exports are man-made. Therefore, I believe, *by showing reverence to a famous mother of scholars,* it emphasizes the importance of education on the Korean society.

38) I recommend for you to go hiking in Korea. Korea has a very mountainous terrain. When you look in almost any direction,

you'll most likely be able to spot a mountain. Going hiking in Korea is one of the most popular hobbies. People enjoy hiking because they can exercise, be in nature, and breathe in fresh air.

Most avid or even amateur hikers in Korea will have hiking shoes, shirts, pants, and a backpack and other accessories.

Typically, you can go hiking with Korean friends all morning and be done in time for lunch. It just depends on how long your planned hike is. This is great fun, and you can enjoy the time with friends and nature.

39) I would recommend walking around the neighborhood. Get to know the local shops. I would recommend walking into the shops and exploring just to get to know what different goods or products they sell. This will help you understand what types of products, foods, and services Koreans appreciate and like.

40) Don't be cheap, especially when you want to build a relationship with people. In Korean culture, it is very common for one individual to pay the entire bill. Instead of splitting the cost of a bill, very often, Koreans will pay the full bill alternatively. For example, I would pay this time, and the other individual will usually offer to pay the following time.

If your meal is 12,000 won and your friend's meal is 18,000 won, it is very common just to cover the full amount. Obviously, it's case by case, but in my experience, I have made many friends not worrying about a few dollars. People like generous people.

This, of course, does not apply with large group outings. Naturally, if you go on a company outing with 12 people, I don't recommend offering to pay the bill's total expense unless you have the financial capacity and willingness to do so.

Common Expression in Korea: Dutch pay or *going Dutch* is when the bill is split between 2 or more people.

This is in contrast with the Korean practice of one person covering the bill in its entirety at a particular time.

41) Koreans are generally very kind. They often may present you a physical gift. Similarly, they often may give you a "verbal gift" in the form of a compliment. They may compliment your shirt, or they may call you handsome or beautiful. Korean people are very generous with their compliments.

Avoid Confusion: However, sometimes their compliments may sound a bit strange if you are unfamiliar with the culture.

They may say "Your nose is so high" or "Your eyes are so big." The "high nose" refers to having a nose bridge that is high. If you have this, then you can imagine that glasses would be able to hang there with ease. Having a low nose-bridge would mean that it would be flatter. In the US, I had never heard of any compliments with regard to someone's nose. I thought it a little funny the first time I heard a nose compliment.

Another common compliment that may seem a bit strange is when a Korean friend says, "Your head is so small." I have been confused when hearing these compliments, but having big eyes, a high nose-bridge, and a small head are seen as attributes of beauty.

> 42) Koreans do not generally hug each other or kiss on the cheek when greeting one another. I would not hug or kiss someone on the cheek after the first meeting because it may be very awkward. A bow or a handshake would be much better.

Cultural hint: In the US, very often, we will give someone a handshake. We are taught to give a firm and energetic handshake. A limp handshake is considered weak and lacking energy.

However, in Korea, I would recommend *lowering the strength and vigor of your grip*. Most Koreans will give a weak handshake, and if you give what is a typical handshake in the US or other countries, it may crush the hand of your new friend.

Therefore, in Korea, I would start the handshake with a weaker grip and strengthen it only if needed. Again, each situation is different and should be viewed as case by case.

43) If a Korean says, "It seems it will be difficult," that generally means "No." This is a Korean way of politely saying No. You have to read between the lines. You'll get better at it as you get more practice.

Cultural Example: Sometimes, it is difficult for people to say No or say the truth. For example, if someone wants to resign from a job, she may say that she has to take care of her parents when the parents may, in fact, not be sick. Others may say they have to focus on their family. They rarely say the truth in these situations.

44) Most fruit in Korea is seasonal. Certain fruit can only be found at certain times of the year. For example, you can usually find strawberries in the springtime. Persimmon, on the other hand, is a fall fruit. This is a good thing. This means that *the fruit you are eating is fresh*. It is most likely not frozen for six months just for it to be available year-round.

Personal experience: When I first arrived in Shinchon in Seoul, I picked up some vegetables and fruit from a street vendor. I grabbed what appeared to me to be tomatoes. Later, I washed the "tomato" and bit into it like an apple. I expected for there to be some resistance from the "tomato". Instead, my bite caused the fruit to cave in, and I got mush all over my face. This sweet, soft stuff was sweet and delicious.

Unbeknownst to me, the "tomato" had actually been a *soft* persimmon. Soft persimmon is called **Hongshi** in Korean. This was my introduction to persimmon. There are other types of persimmon.

Hard persimmon is call **DanGam.**

Last, persimmon can also be *dried*. This is called **KodGam.** Just as a grape turns into a raisin when dried, Persimmon becomes KodGam when dried. It is the same fruit in a different state, so we give it another name.

45) Every fall in Korea, there are a few certainties. The leaves of the trees become colorful, and it is a season when Koreans enjoy hiking. Those are the pleasant things associated with the autumn. In addition to those things, the female ginkgo trees drop their nuts on the streets of major cities, and they leave an awful rotting smell. This is one unpleasant part of the fall. The odor of this ginkgo tree is absolutely hideous and is unmistakable. These gingko nuts are tasty when cooked. However, when they are left to rot on the street, their odor is straight-up foul. You will probably see some older Korean women, or **ajumas**, shaking the tree and gathering the fallen nuts. This is a win-win situation. They can use the nuts in their

cooking. Most importantly, you will not have to smell that awful smell the next time you pass by that tree.

46) Something that I found fascinating was that most Koreans have cars in one of three colors: white black or gray. I was wondering why, and a Korean friend told me that the cars in those colors have a higher resale value in Korea. You will notice this when you look at a street full of cars.

47) Try the sashimi and sushi in Korea. It is excellent. Especially, the seafood is extra fresh by the sea or seaside cities. You can usually go to a fish market and ask for them to prepare fresh sashimi for you on the spot. It will be a lot less costly than having it at a restaurant, so you can eat more for the same price, or you can eat the same amount for a lot less money. Eating out in Korea is a lot cheaper than in other countries. However, if you want to eat sashimi in a restaurant, it is usually not cheap. Therefore, I highly recommend having it prepared from the fish market and eating it with friends. **This is what the locals do!**

48) Learn the right way to eat with chopsticks. You should hold them from a high position. As soon as you arrive in Korea, you should ask a friend how to use the chopsticks appropriately.

Before you model them, ask them if they hold it the way they should be held. If they hold them from a middle position (Yes, even some Koreans do this), it will look child-like. I hold the chopsticks from a high position, which is seen as the proper handling of chopsticks. This will *earn you credibility* in the Korean and Asian community!

Food etiquette: Usually, rice is eaten with a spoon. I tried to show off and used chopsticks to eat the rice, but it's usually a waste of time trying to grab those individual grains with chopsticks. Noodles, on the other hand, are always eaten with chopsticks.

49) Waste here is different. In the US, for example, food is combined with general waste. In Korea, the food waste goes with the food waste. What this means is that there will be a bin outside your apartment building that is specifically dedicated for food waste. General waste goes in the general waste bin. Then you will see that cardboard or paper goes in one bin. Plastic recyclables go in another bin. There will most likely be a bin for glass and one for Styrofoam. Last but not least, you will also have to dispose of your plastic bag in which you carry the food waste in. There is also a small waste bag filled with these dirty plastic bags.

Useful hint: I noticed some locals use a *plastic glove* to open the lids of the bins. This way, they avoid having to touch those nasty lids.

50) Quite often, the focus of a mother is to educate the children. Therefore, a lot of parenting in Korea is just delegating the education and sending the kids to the best schools they can get into. After their school day is finished, then the mothers will spend time driving their kids to after-school academies. Otherwise, the kids may be able to take a bus by themselves.

Many parents have good intentions and do this because they feel that they are not the experts. For example, in math they delegate the math education to someone better qualified. This can be great parenting.

On the other hand, I suspect that many other parents send their kids to academies to pretend like they care. They are merely trying to show that they are being good parents. The other reason they send their kids to academies is because they don't really want to watch their kids. This is my personal opinion.

I know *many Korean mothers are wonderful!* But other mothers are just going through the motions. They simply want to find a babysitter at the academy and free up their time to chat with friends at the coffee shop or go practice golf or any other hobby. I'm not trying to hate, and I don't blame them. I'm just observing and writing down what I saw.

51) Koreans are a very kind people. Don't be surprised if they share a gift or some food with you. Quite often, as a private tutor, I was gifted food or gifts. After teaching, sometimes the student or the student's parent would give me some sweet potatoes or some tangerines for me to take home. This is not uncommon. Also, for Teacher's Day, there were times when I received socks, after-shave, or some other practical gift. Really, Koreans can be very generous!

Cultural Note: Christmas is a *gift-giving* holiday in America where we usually exchange gifts with family members and loved ones. In the US, Christmas is widely seen as a holiday that you spend with family. However, In Korea, it's not a traditional holiday. Also, it has a different meaning.

It is mostly seen as a day when couples get together and go on a date. It's not seen as a family day. Still, for Christians, it's an important holiday and families may gather to go to church. In general, though, you will hear people ask one another if they have any dates planned, or they will talk about how they wish they had someone special in their life.

52) When a Korean gets a promotion or when something good happens to them, they often *spread the happiness with friends*,

and it's quite common for them to treat their friends to a coffee, a drink or a meal.

53) Getting a haircut in Korea is great. You still do have to find someone who cuts hair well. The old adage still applies-_**Never see a young doctor or an old barber.**_ In fact, I only saw a barber once when I first went there in 2002. It was at a place called the Blue Club because they gave $5 haircuts. After the 2 minutes, I knew that I had overpaid, to my dismay. That was my first and worst experience getting a haircut in Korea. I don't think I was acquainted with the adage at that time.

After that, almost all my haircuts in Korea were very good. Before you get a haircut in Korea, they will usually ask you if you want to wash your hair. This is usually at no additional cost. Unless I had just showered, _I always took the free hair wash._ Sometimes they will massage your scalp a bit. It feels really good. Then the young hair stylist will cut your hair, and after the haircut, she will ask you if you want to wash again. This is so you don't walk around with hair all over your neck or shirt.

This second wash is _also free of charge_. Afterward, you will return to your chair, and they will dry it and style it for you if you want. All this for a sum of 12,000 won and no tip is needed. **Again, do not tip!** It is unnecessary and not expected. The hair stylist receives a monthly salary, and no tip is needed. Again, I would pay this much money in 2014. This is for a man's haircut. Obviously, prices differ depending on the neighborhood and whether it is a haircut for a man or a woman, and it also depends on what style or product you request. Overall, you will most likely be impressed with the quality and price of haircuts in Korea, but keep in mind the adage, and it does depend on your hair stylist's skill level.

> 54) *Korea is not a mingling culture.* In general, Koreans will not have house parties where they invite many different groups of friends and all the people have an opportunity to bounce from group to group "mingling". In my years of living in Korea, this did not happen one time.

In the US, there are often house parties or barbeques in which people may find themselves mingling (standing) with strangers or people that they just met for the first time. In Korea, this never happens.

In contrast, Koreans usually don't meet in each other's homes. They usually meet in a public place, such as a coffee shop, and they almost always gather in a seated position. If they meet someone new, the new person is usually introduced by an existing member of the group.

Personal Note: When I returned from Korea, I was living with my family. We visited my aunt's house because she was having a barbeque. Most of my family was standing and talking. Some were having a beer while others were sitting and eating. This environment **_with my family_** felt very awkward. In my near decade of living in Korea, all the gatherings that I attended were ones where everyone was seated. Therefore, even though I was with my family, I still felt uncomfortable because of the "mingling" setting.

Second Thought: The only exception that I could come up with is at a club. Usually, at clubs, everyone "mingles". This usually happens with much greater ease and intoxication, not necessarily in that order.

> 55) Since Korea is not a mingling country, they must have different ways to meet new people, right?

Yes, you are absolutely right. The way they do it is through an intermediary. It's actually quite common for Koreans to ask a friend for a **"Sogaeting"**. A "Sogaeting" is a hook-up. For example, let's just say that a woman named Mary is friends with Tim, but she also has a friend named Michelle. If Tim would like to go on a date with Michelle, he will not ask her out directly. Instead, he will ask Mary if she could set them up on a "Sogaeting". It's really common for Korean couples to have met through a mutual acquaintance or friend. *This is a big part of the culture.*

Practical use: If you are looking to date in Korea, you can simply ask a Korean friend "Can you set me up on a Sogaeting?" Simple, right?

> 56) Koreans often meet people through a match-maker. This has been part of the culture for a long time. This is not limited to dating. This method for meeting someone is also used for meeting a potential marriage partner. When someone wants to get married, she will often go to a "**Sun-Boda**". This is a date through match-making with the intent of finding a partner for marriage. When they enroll for this "Sun-Boda" service, they answer questions about what type of individual they are looking for. This helps the match-maker arrange for potential ideal partners.

This is just an opportunity to meet someone. Naturally, if one of the persons does not like the other, then there will be no match. Both parties have to like or love one another for it to be considered a match. Individuals can go on "Sun-Boda" dates until they are satisfied. This is very different from arranged marriages in which there is no choice for either individual.

These dates are arranged by a match-maker, who tries to match two individuals usually by certain specifications. The specifications may involve height, weight, build, or they may involve something like where they attended university or their occupation.

For example, a woman may say, "I want to meet a doctor who is at least 6ft tall and from a family with substantial financial assets." Any combination of factors can be chosen, but it's still no guarantee they can be found. Even worse, if found, still that is no guarantee the person will like or love you.

Finally, when there is a match, the couple usually arranges the wedding plans, and they get married. Again, this is not guaranteed and to have success in marriage is something that needs work and some luck, too.

57) When a couple is dating in Korea, most likely, they will not introduce one another to their parents. I remember, before I went to Korea, when my parents were both alive, I introduced them to my girlfriends. There was no extreme pressure, and those meetings didn't have extraordinary or crucial significance. Please take this with a grain of salt because I was in my late teens or early twenties at that time. Most relationships then were not that serious. Also, my previous girlfriends did not have any hesitation introducing me to their parents.

Nonetheless, each culture is different, and the same can be said for Korea.

In Korea, I had a few girlfriends, and *I was never introduced to their parents*. We had never been serious about marriage. Therefore, they would not introduce me to their parents. That was fine by me, too. Most Koreans would not introduce their partners to their parents *until they are both ready to get married* and it's agreed that they should take the step of being introduced to each other's parents. When I finally met my girlfriend's parents, they were the parents of my future wife.

58) The word **Yak-Sok** literally means an appointment. It is a generic word that means you have plans. If a Korean friend says they have a *yak-sok,* that means they have plans, and they will not be able to meet you that day. The verb to do a *Yak-sok* can mean *to promise*, as in "*I promise* we'll go out to lunch together after I finish my tests."

59) One of the *best things of Korea* is the **access to medical care.** There are small clinics everywhere in Korea. It's a great thing that this is a study-culture because it seems to foster a great environment to produce quality doctors.

There are two reasons I love medical service in Korea. First, you don't need an appointment, and they will attend you the same day. Second, the cost is relatively cheap. Compared with the US, the cost and time difference is not even close. Korea is far more easily available, and you can walk into a clinic with no appointment and be attended the same day. Also, if you have insurance, a regular visit to the doctor may cost you a few thousand won, which amounts to a few US dollars. If you have no insurance, then the cost for a regular visit may be around 15,000 won or around US $15.00.

Again, even with no insurance, it is often much cheaper to get medical or dental care in Korea than it is in the US even with insurance. When I visit Korea, I usually get a general health and dental check-up. This is mainly because the quality and price are both good.

Many Koreans who live abroad visit Korea regularly at least once a year to take care of their overall health and teeth. They will also take care of any medical or cosmetic needs or wants they may have.

Inside Korea: If you want insurance, as a foreigner, you get can medical insurance and be covered.

All Korean citizens are covered under the national medical insurance. This grants them access to affordable and comprehensive health care. Because of this, when Koreans get sick, there is absolutely no hesitation, and they visit a doctor. I think this is a MAJOR CONTRIBUTOR to the *high standard of living* in Korea.

60) The holidays in Korea are marked on the calendars by the color red. Some are based on the calendar that we use, which is based on the sun. For example, **Children's Day**, will always fall on

May 5th of the year. However, the biggest holidays in Korea are based on the lunar calendar. Therefore, those holidays *move* on the solar calendar (the one we use). For example, the biggest holiday may be **New Year's Day**. This holiday falls on the 1st day of the year *using the Lunar Calendar*. However, since the Lunar Calendar and the Solar Calendar have a different number of days (12 lunar months equals around 354 solar calendar days), the lunar-calendar based holidays will fall on different days each year.

For example, Lunar New Year will fall on January 25th, 2020, but the following year (2021), it will fall on February 12th.

61) During the red days of **Chuseok**, or the *Korean Thanksgiving* and during the **Lunar New Year,** the whole country is moving and people are returning to their hometowns. They are returning to meet with their family members or to visit their parents. Since there is a mass movement during and prior to these holidays, I strongly recommend for you to *book your transportation* needs at least *2 or 3 weeks before the holiday*. This will ensure you actually get tickets. Sometimes, tickets can be sold-out during this time, so to avoid the hassle during the long holidays, make sure you book your transportation needs in advance.

62) Expect the manners to be different. Many things in Korea are good. These things that I'm going to mention are not particularly good. When you sneeze, you just sneeze. Nobody says, "God bless you." This one, I don't mind. What I do mind is when someone else sneezes or coughs and he doesn't cover his mouth.

Koreans often do not cover their mouths when they cough, so be aware of this and just get out of the way and hold your breath. That way, whatever they cough-up, hopefully, doesn't enter your body. I'm not a doctor, but that's the best way I can think of to avoid somebody else's cough explosion.

Also, it is very crowded in many places in Korea, so you will get bumped into. The common thing for the bumper to do is simply to *bump-and-go*. Koreans often will not say, "excuse me" or "sorry". I imagine that the younger generation may be better mannered as they are more acquainted with travel and different cultures.

Another common occurrence will happen when you are entering a shop, and someone is just 3 steps ahead of you. They will most likely open the door slightly, just enough so they can get through, and let it slam on you. Don't expect Koreans to hold the door for you. This was especially true while I was living in Korea (until 2014) and before. On a recent visit (2019), I did notice that they had a sticker on a department store's front door with the writing "Please hold door for the next person." I was happily surprised. The department store was educating the customers on door manners. Perhaps by the time you read this, you won't have the door shut on you when you are trailing someone entering a building.

63) One thing that I think is a huge benefit to life in Korea is that there are no guns in Korea. There is little civilian gun-ownership in Korea. Koreans may own guns only for sport or hunting, but there are strict laws they have to follow. In general, though, most Koreans can't and don't own a gun. I know this may scare a lot of Americans or people from other countries. However, for me, it's a big advantage. First of all, I don't even own a gun in the US. Therefore, I have never directly benefited from guns. Second, to me, it seems like there is a great benefit from knowing that other people are not carrying guns. I feel a lot safer living in Korea than I do in the US. One major reason is that civilian gun-ownership is close to being banned in Korea.

Additional information: Just because Koreans don't own guns doesn't mean they can't use them. In fact, most Korean males learn how to use guns when they do their mandatory military training.

64) The Korean police is not intimidating at all. This is a good thing. I know the police in America have a very difficult job, and the police work very hard, but in my opinion, the police here can be intimidating. The police in Korea don't seem to look for things to get you with. I'm fortunate and have not encountered the police much in the US, but still I find them to be intimidating. In Korea, if a police car is trailing you, it doesn't have much meaning. In the US, people immediately get out of the way to avoid possibly getting pulled over. At least, that's what I typically do here. With the Korean police, I don't feel any sort of intimidation. Maybe it's just me, but that's how I feel.

Another thing I noticed is that, in Korea, the cars don't yield for ambulances or fire trucks during an emergency. Many cars just continue on their ordinary path with no thought of yielding to the emergency vehicles. With this, I think the US does it better. We should yield in case of an emergency because someone's life can be saved by yielding to the rescuers.

65) Walkers beware! I don't know the official rules, but I do know what happens when I'm in the streets of Korea. Anytime you are outside walking and there is a car being driven and you are

going to cross paths, then stop right there and expect for the car to go. If you don't stop, you will get hit. Cars do not yield for the pedestrians like they do in America.

In the US, there are so many traffic signs that say, "Yield to Pedestrians." These signs are usually followed. In Korea, you should be more careful. The car will NOT slow down. Always expect the hasty drivers to go and not wait for you to cross. This obviously is not a plus if you are a walker. However, it's better to wait than to get hit. Just be aware that *in practice* in Korea, **the cars have the right of way!**

66) In Korea *age is very important*! You will be asked your age over and over. In fact, it's very difficult to have a relationship with someone in Korea unless you know one another's age. One reason age is important is because Confucianism influenced Korean culture tremendously. One of the principles of Confucianism is that you should respect your elders.

Furthermore, Korea has different types of speech. You use Honorifics or respectful language when you speak with someone who is older than you. Also, if the person is a stranger, you will default to using respectful language.

However, if you know the person well and they are younger than you, then you may use informal language.

A big part of *how you speak to someone is dependent on the age of the listener*. Therefore, as a Korean, if you want to speak with someone, you will have to know their age. This is why Koreans will undoubtedly ask you about your age.

Additional tip about age: In Korean culture, only if you were born the same year as someone can you be considered a *Chin-gu,* which means friend. If you are one year older than someone, then that younger person will call you "older sister" or "older brother", not friend.

67) One way that Koreans show their love is by giving. Usually, in small shops or if you buy from a market, the vendors may throw in an additional good and say "Service". In this case, "Service" means "on the house" or "at no additional charge". This is a Korean word with its origin coming from English. Obviously, the original meaning has been changed from "the way you take care of your customer" to "this food or item is on the house."

For example, if you are at a pub and you order some alcoholic beverages and some food, after some time, workers may give shots for everyone and say, "service". They are simply giving shots free of charge.

Practical use: In Korea, if you shop at a market, you can negotiate. You can ask for a "DC", which is short for **dis**count in Korean. This also is derived from English. The meaning is the same.

Ex: If you find something you like at the market, you can ask, "Can you DC?"

This grammatically incorrect sentence will most likely be understood. The vendor will understand this incorrect usage of English. *Plus, you might get a discount!*

> 68) In Korean, ***Pob*** means rice. But ***Pob*** also means meal. This is because rice is associated with a meal in Korea. If you want to have a proper meal in Korea, then you *must have rice!* Therefore, the two words rice and a meal are somewhat synonymous in Korea.

Many Koreans consider having a sandwich being an improper meal. For it to be considered a meal, there must be rice.

Cultural note: "Did you have Rice?" can also be used as a greeting. It can mean "How are you?" The phrase comes from the time after the Korean war *when food was scarce*. If you had had rice, it meant that you were alive and doing well.

Personal story: I went to the gym one day. When the trainer asked me, "Hello Mancho, did you have Pob?" I answered, "No, I had a chicken sandwich." He looked surprised as he laughed. That's when I learned that he wasn't asking what I had for dinner. It was more or less a greeting like, "How are you?"

69) In Korea, there is major pressure for women to get married before the age of 30. Parents will usually pester their daughters around the age of 28 or 29 and begin to ask when they are getting married. This sometimes gives women around that age huge pressure. This is not a hard rule, but it is a general practice by most parents. I don't know why 30 is the number, but that's kind of an unwritten rule in Korean society. It can be a burden to 28- and 29-year-old women.

70) Although the rates have been increasing, and it's actually quite common, *divorce is seen as very negative in Korea*. I was quite surprised because most divorced people in Korea seem to be really embarrassed or somewhat ashamed over having been divorced. It is seen as much worse than in the US. In the US, you can be divorced multiple times, and it's your choice. It may just not have worked out between two people.

In Korea, however, people try to keep quiet about it till this day. Truthfully, if I was a divorced Korean, I would really consider living abroad, or at least I would start spending more time abroad to be able to live with peace of mind.

71) In my opinion, Korea is a great country in which to live. That was my personal experience. However, Koreans do face a lot of pressure at times. Students have pressure to perform well in school. Husbands have a lot of pressure to produce economically for the family. In addition to that, Korea is a country where respect and honor are very important. Also, more so than in the US, I feel that people are more judgmental. Particularly, because there are so many people living in such a small space. As a result of all these factors and others, Korea has a very high suicide rate.

72) Koreans drink a lot of alcohol. There are a lot of places where people drink. Usually, there are company outings where workers are kind of pressured to drink alcohol. Besides that, Koreans will drink with their friends or family. Bars and restaurants are open until late every night, so you will find many places to drink. Beware if you go to a Korean-styled night club (AKA Booking Night Club) where you are seated and they bring guys or gals to your table. For men, you must buy an expensive bottle of alcohol that comes with fruit. The bottle with the fruit usually costs around US $150. For women, you can go there more cheaply.

73) There are various types of alcohol. Amongst them, some of the most popular are beer, soju, and makgeolli. Beer is already known. Koreans brew their own kind of beer. On the other hand, Soju is a Korean alcoholic beverage that tastes a little like vodka. However, it's much cheaper than vodka. People love it in Korea, and usually the most popular brand will depend on the region where you live. Each region has traditionally had a representative soju. Finally, makgeolli is an alcoholic beverage made from rice. It's kind of a rice wine.

74) Be careful when walking on the sidewalks. Sometimes, *if you hear a roar of an engine behind you and the sound is getting louder and louder, it's probably a scooter* or small motorcycle that's used for delivery. I remember this used to bother me a lot because I always felt that it was dangerous, and those vehicles should be on the road! They should not be on the sidewalk. But then I realized that I just need to get out of the way when that happens. I would just move aside until the scooter flew right past me on the sidewalk. It's an inconvenience and danger to us, but I recommend that you do the same and get out of the way until they pass.

Useful hint: One thing that's fantastic about Korea is that you can be in a park, and you can call a food place, and they will deliver to the park. They will ride the scooters into the park area and drop it off anywhere you request. **You must get delivery in Korea in a park.**

75) *Plastic surgery in Korea is very common.* In fact, there are many cases where a teenager may not want any surgery, but the parents want them to get the surgery. In other cases, the person will take initiative and seek surgery on their own accord. The most common type of surgery is making the double eye-lid. Koreans, in general, care more about the face than the body. Therefore, more often than not, the surgeries are on the face. But I must say that recently Koreans have been placing more and more emphasis on their bodies than in the past.

76) Just like General Tso's chicken is only found in Chinese-American food, there is such a thing as Chinese-Korean food. Food like General Tso's chicken was created by a Chinese person living in America. Therefore, it is really only eaten in the US. Chinese people who live in China have never heard of General Tso's Chicken.

There are also Chinese people living in Korea. The Korean-Chinese foods that are the most popular are probably Tang-Soo-Yook and Jja-Jang-Myun. Tang-Soo-Yook is sweet and sour pork. Jja-Jang-Myun are black-bean paste noodles. Jja-Jang-Myun is a dish created by a

Chinese person living in Korea. It is not a Chinese dish. Anyway, wherever it's from, it's tasty!

77) Prior to going to Korea, I had no idea what my *blood type* was. Then, I was asked over and over, "What is your blood type?" You would think that I urgently had to do a blood transfusion in the following days or something. No, that wasn't the case. What I later found out is that Koreans think there is a relation with your blood type and your personality. What they really want to know is if you're friendly and open or if you have psychotic tendencies according to your blood-type.

Practical Tip: I found out my blood type through luck in the US prior to going to Korea. At my workplace one day, I donated blood to a blood bank, and they gave me a blood donor's card that had my blood type on it.

If you learn your blood type, *find out if you're the* **psycho** *or the* **easy-going person** because you will be asked. Whatever the result is, have fun with it.

78) Have you ever noticed Koreans taking pictures? Do you ever see the peace sign with the palms facing the camera? If you spend time in Korea, for some reason, you may begin to do this when taking a picture. If you find yourself doing it, then *you are becoming* more and more Korean.

79) *Ondol* is the name of the heating system that is used in Korea where the heat comes from underneath the floors. This traditional way of heating keeps your house or room warm for an extended period of time.

Bonus: They say that cold travels quickly through the feet. With *ondol,* your floors will be heated, and it will help keep your feet and body warmer.

80) When you are walking down the streets in Korea, you may notice some young couples wearing a "Couple Shirt". This simply means that a couple wears the same shirt to show that they are together as a couple in unity.

Challenge: If you wear a couple-shirt in Korea, you will become the ultimate-Korean!

I will absolutely marvel at your excellency in conforming to the culture.

81) If you want to hang out with or see a Korean friend, but they have a test, expect not to see them *until after* the test. As mentioned earlier, studying is a big deal in Korea. When someone has an important test coming up, they solely focus on the test. Koreans try to limit distractions when facing an important test. The best thing to do if your friend has a test is

to find out the test date and contact your friend after the test is done.

Inside Scoop in the Korean mind: *During test times, all other activities must cease*!

82) There is such a thing in Korea called the **Hyu-Hak (break from studies)**, which we call a gap-year. A *Hyu-Hak*, which is usually done at some point in university, is a gap-year that many college students use in order to go abroad for a year and improve their English. This has become more and more popular as Koreans enjoy foreign travel and feel the need to improve their English abilities in order to be more marketable in the job-market.

Made in the USA
Las Vegas, NV
22 February 2022